Imaginations

Book 3

By Kevin Olson

Intermediate

Notes from the Composer

I find it interesting that we use the word "keys" to describe the black and white levers on the piano that are pressed down and transformed into musical art. It's as if musicians have always understood that the piano has the ability to unlock our creativity and imagination. With these eighty-eight keys, pianists can open doors to new colors, images, and ideas, first by playing inspirational music by other composers, and eventually composing original pieces. I have used the keys on my own piano to come up with a variety of solos in this collection, exploring new pathways of my own imagination. I hope these pieces will inspire you to unlock the amazing potential of your own imagination.

Kevin Olson

Contents

Tales from Madrid

Kevin Olson

6

Above and Beyond

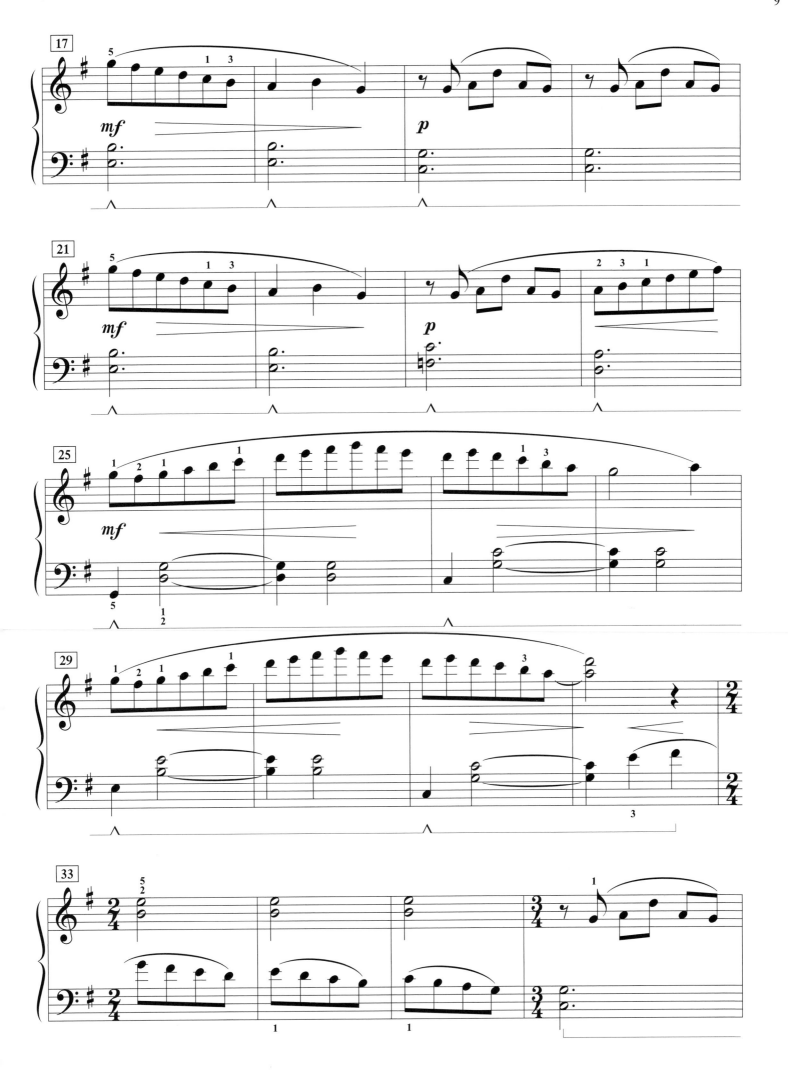

Carousel

Elegant waltz tempo (♩ = ca. 136)

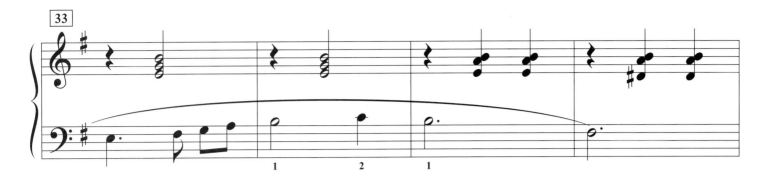

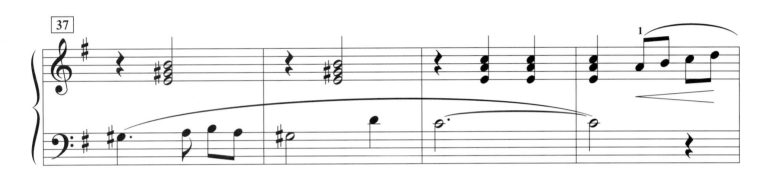

14

High Five

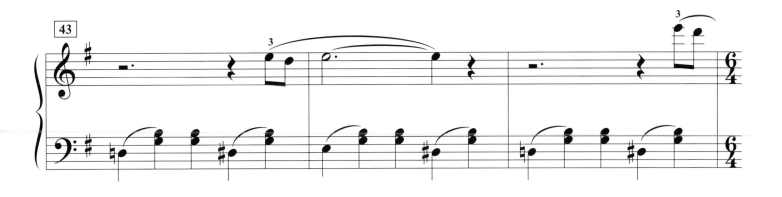

Color the World

Expressively; freely (♩ = ca. 104)

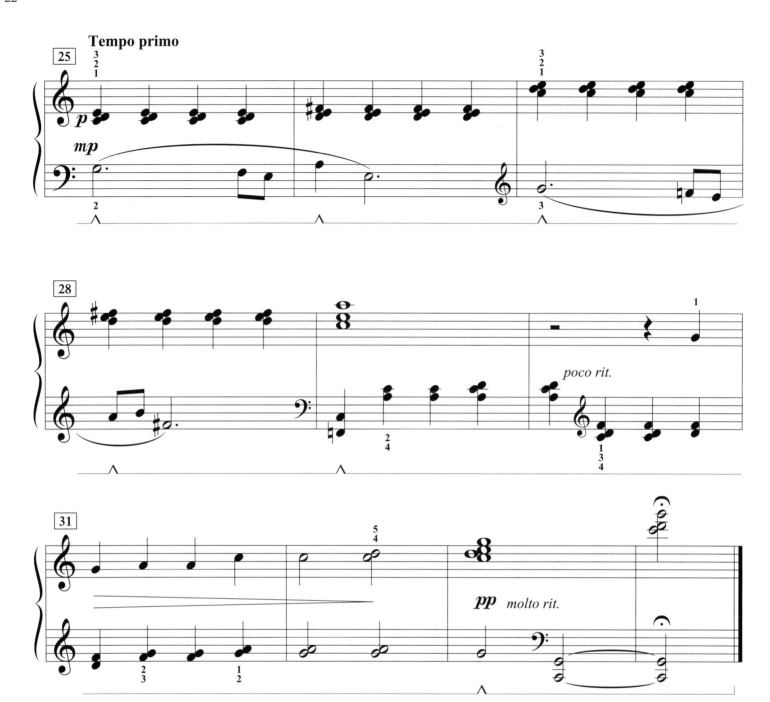

dedicated to Julia for our 22nd wedding anniversary

Love Notes

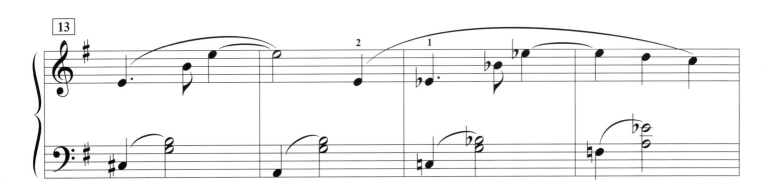

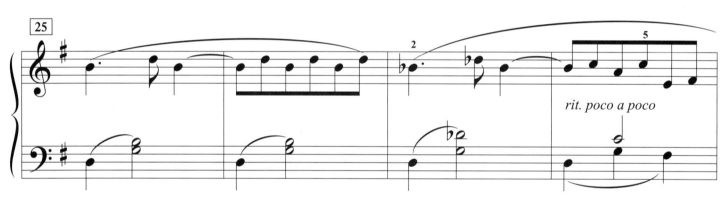

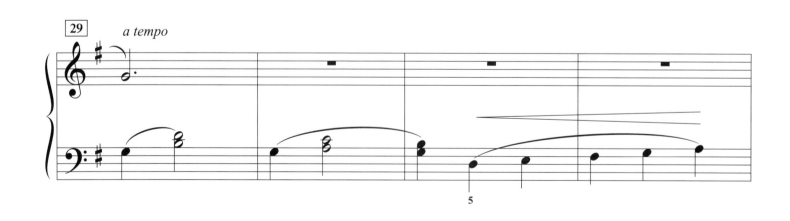

26

FJH2318

Power Chords

With a heavy rock beat (♩ = ca. 152)